HAL•LEONARD
INSTRUMENTAL PLAY-ALONG

AUDIO ACCESS INCLUDED

PLAYBACK+
Speed • Pitch • Balance • Loop

CLARINET

Movie and TV Music

Audio Arrangements by Peter Deneff

To access audio visit:
www.halleonard.com/mylibrary
Enter Code
2281-0173-7384-2155

ISBN 978-1-5400-2063-5

HAL•LEONARD®

Visit Hal Leonard Online at
www.halleonard.com

Contact Us:
Hal Leonard
7777 West Bluemound Road
Milwaukee, WI 53213
Email: info@halleonard.com

In Europe contact:
Hal Leonard Europe Limited
Distribution Centre, Newmarket Road
Bury St Edmunds, Suffolk, IP33 3YB
Email: info@halleonardeurope.com

In Australia contact:
Hal Leonard Australia Pty. Ltd.
4 Lentara Court
Cheltenham, Victoria, 3192 Australia
Email: info@halleonard.com.au

THE AVENGERS

from THE AVENGERS

Clarinet

Composed by
ALAN SILVESTRI

CAPTAIN AMERICA MARCH

from CAPTAIN AMERICA

CLARINET

By ALAN SILVESTRI

DOCTOR WHO XI

CLARINET

By MURRAY GOLD

DOWNTON ABBEY
(Theme)

Clarinet

Music by JOHN LUNN

GAME OF THRONES
Theme from the HBO Series GAME OF THRONES

By RAMIN DJAWADI

CLARINET

GUARDIANS OF THE GALAXY

from GUARDIANS OF THE GALAXY

Clarinet

Composed by TYLER BATES,
DIETER HARTMANN, TIMOTHY WILLIAMS
and KURT OLDMAN

HAWAII FIVE-O THEME
from the Television Series

CLARINET

By MORT STEVENS

MARRIED LIFE

from UP

CLARINET

By MICHAEL GIACCHINO

OUTLANDER THEME
(The Skye Boat Song)

CLARINET

Traditional Music
Arranged by BEAR McCREARY

PROLOGUE AND PROLOGUE PART 2

from BEAUTY AND THE BEAST

Clarinet

REY'S THEME
from STAR WARS: THE FORCE AWAKENS

CLARINET

Music by JOHN WILLIAMS

THEME FROM THE X-FILES

from the Twentieth Century Fox Television Series THE X-FILES

CLARINET

By MARK SNOW

TEST DRIVE

from the Motion Picture HOW TO TRAIN YOUR DRAGON

CLARINET

By JOHN POWELL